A Big Move

by Elise Walters

illustrated by Bill Peterson

PEARSON

Scott Foresman

Editorial Offices: Glenview, Illinois • Parsippany, New Jersey • New York, New York
Sales Offices: Needham, Massachusetts • Duluth, Georgia • Glenview, Illinois
Coppell, Texas • Sacramento, California • Mesa, Arizona

Mom got a new job.

Mom and I had to move away.

Mom got boxes at a store.

Mom and I packed our things.

Mom got some ads.

Mom and I looked for

a new house.

Mom saw a very big house
by a school.
Mom and I said it's fine for us.

Mom watches from the car.

Mom and I will miss our friends.

People often move from one place to another place. Sometimes these places are close together. But many times people move far away to a whole new country. Millions of people come to the United States from other countries. Many of them arrive first in New York City. When they get there, they are greeted by a famous symbol of freedom, the Statue of Liberty.